JUN TSUJI (1884-1944):
THE DADA SCRIBBLINGS

Jun Tsuji (1884 - 1944) was born in Tokyo, Japan, in the district of Asakusa. He was a writer of essays, poetry, and plays; a translator of Oscar Wilde, Cesare Lombroso, Thomas de Quincey, and Max Stirner; sometime stage actor and political activist; a musician and bohemian lifestylist.

Ryan Choi's books include *Three Demons: A Study on Sanki Saitō's Haiku* and *In Dreams & Other Stories: The Very Short Stories of Ryūnosuke Akutagawa*. He is an editor at *AGNI*. His writings and translations have appeared in *Harper's Magazine, The New Criterion, Poetry, Times Literary Supplement*, and elsewhere. He lives in Honolulu, Hawai'i, where he was born and raised.

ISBN: 978-1-917617-19-2

Cover designed by Aaron Kent

Edited and Typeset by Aaron Kent

Broken Sleep Books Ltd
PO BOX 102
Llandysul
SA44 9BG

CONTENTS

【あぶさるど】   8

ABSOLUTE   9

【タンカ】   12

TANKA   13

【闇汁】   16

DARKNESS STEW   17

【どうおなりでしょう】   24

WHAT HAS BECOME, WILL BECOME   25

【無題詩】   26

UNTITLED I   27

【無題】   28

UNTITLED II   29

【タンカ】   30

TANKA II   31

【享楽座」のぷろろぐ】   36

PROLOGUE TO "THE THEATRE OF PLEASURE"   37

ACKNOWLEDGEMENTS   45

For my father

The Dada Scribblings

Jun Tsuji
Translated by Ryan Choi

Broken Sleep Books

【あぶさるど】

転覆、逆上、生命の捩じれ
度外れた哄笑、娼婦の白血球
駱駝の鈍感……豹の電流を注射しろ
バットの吸殻を拾う……ボロボロボ
赤練ガを焼いて■■■■におつっけろ
呼吸器械の喘ぎ……開かれた■
三百代言の首を■■■!!
狂人の真っ蒼に爛れた舌
麻痺した神経を硫酸で焼き尽せ
■■した犬の苦笑
接点は接点だ……
無限に楕円を描け、無限に転回しろ
生命の浪費は涎を垂らしている
ポコ　ポコ　ポコ　ポコ
凹凸　凸凹　凸ボコ　ボコ
ピストンの欠伸に触れるな
ブリキ板の方がお前の胸より柔らかい
血が青白く流れて、滴っている
ポタリ　ポタリ……タリ　タリ……
月が赤く笑っている
狂犬の死体を咬るスタカト
梟の眼は黒曜石よりも素晴らしい
逆さにつるされた胴体
風の残酷なフリュウトがきこえてきた
闇……大きなうつろな穴

1924

ABSOLUTE

Overthrow; unrest; existential parody;
obnoxious, inappropriate guffawing; slut leukocytes;
camel dumb head—*electric panther injection,*

scavenging for butts on the seafloor—worn,
       torn
       rumblings. Burn
the lacquered red atman sketches—
       songs of moths, congratulatory
       ditties—package
and mail the ashes to ____. Wheezing

of mechanical respirators, ligatured, spread-
       eagled on _____ racks.

___ the conmen's heads!—their tongues: festering,
       inflamed
       lunatic blue: acidize their palsied

       nerves—*dogs*, who ____, and fake

grin-stuck candor.

Tangent point is *the tangent point.*

Carve the ellipse on the infinity canvas,

(rotate). *Then, rotate again.*

("*Life of a Wastrel*," summed at his toes in a lake of drool.)

Ess   Ess   Ess   Ess
Craterous Coarseness Coarse-ness Ness

PISTONS YAWNING, *don't touch!—*

        tin sheets softer than teats, bluish-white blood
flowing from tips—slowing to
        a drip,
dripping dripping ping ping

RED MOON, grinning (staccato): *gnawing on*

        rabies warm dog-corpses.

Eyes of OWL—more

        magnificent
        than obsidian—cold

bodies hung by purpled
ankles—fluyts

aired by brutish winds—

darkness......*a gaping.*

1924

【タンカ】

雲を喰らい、霞を呑んでいるとでも
大方思っていやがるのだろう
ゴミのような雑誌に
ロハで原稿を書かせやがって
往復ハガキさえよこせば
キット返事をよこすものだと
思っていやがる　ヒョットコメ!!
おれは毎日水をガブガブと呑んで
その辺の野原から雑草をひきぬいて
ナマでムシャムシャ食っているのだが
──別段クタバリもしない
一度や二度飯が食えないと
もうふるえあがりやがって
黄色いシナビタ声を張りあげやがって
ナンダカンダと抜かしやがる
スットコドッコイのトンチキ野郎の
ヒョットコメ!!
ガツガツと、物欲しそうなそのツラは
全体なんといううざまだ!!
いい気になってつけあがりやがって
やれ、ムサンケイキュウだの
ブルジョアだのと
阿保の一つ覚えみていなよまいごとを
よくあきもせず、性コリもなく
ツベコベツベコベと饒舌りやがる
デクの棒の、アヤツリ人形の
猿真似の、賤民野郎め!!

12

TANKA

"Scarfing down clouds and sucking up mist..."

As a whole, I loathe the thought of this,

      just as I loathe the thought of publishing

In *RUBBISH* magazines for *FREE*,

Even if they *SINCERELY* honor

      my *EXISTENCE*

      with the return postcards
I send with my scripts—what

      an *UGLY CLOWN FACE*

      that is me!

Every day I gulp water, yank weeds
From the field across the road,

      and *MUNCH* on them raw.

It doesn't particularly *KILL* me—

If I don't eat once or twice a day
I get the shakes and yap random

      phrases in *PUBLIC*

In my *XANTHOUS,* wilted voice:

"Yes, I'm the *DEPRAVED IDIOT* knave,

cursed with the *UGLY CLOWN FACE!*"

—whose hideous, piggish, greedy expression

is the shame of *ALL EARTH*...

YET LOOK:

the *BOURGEOISIE,*

spoiled rotten and living leisurely—

SUDDENLY BEREFT OF PROPERTY

they are nothing but desperate
Complainers, tirelessly *GRUMBLING*

and *GRUMBLING* about

their one loss worth remembering...

WOODEN puppets, with *MANIPULABLE*

STICKS for spines,

Poorly aping the wretched *PROLETARIAT!*

【闇汁】

というものは食べたことがありませんが、
多分こんなものだと思っています。
昔ギリシアの子供達が、燕が初めて飛んでくる時に
町の中を戸毎に唄って歩いたという歌でも御紹介いたしましょうか?
おいで、おいで、燕さん
美しい春がやって来ましたね
燕ときれいなお天気が一緒に来ます
燕さんの胸が白くって、あとはみんな
真っ黒け
僕らにお菓子を投げて下さい
あなたの家のおくらから
燕さんのために御報謝
お酒はフラスコの中
チーズはバスケットの中
小麦のパンと烏麦のパン
燕さんが嬉しがりますよ
さあ、あなた方が下さるか、僕らが
先へ行くか?
なぜ、そんなにグズグズしているの?
イヤならイヤでよござんす
この戸を外して持ってゆきますよ
そんなことはズイブンやさしい
家の中のおかみさんがチビだから
さあ、サッサとお出しなさい
燕のために戸を開けろ
僕らは子供で
おじいちゃんじゃないのだよ

DARKNESS STEW

is something I have never tasted,

but, if I had to guess, it tastes something like this—

"*Students*, let us refer to the children's
        song sung *thura* to

            thura in Ancient
Greece

to herald the appearance of the swallows:

      Come out,
            spring has arrived!

      Open the gynaikon windows!

      Swallows fly in blue skies!

      See the black plumes, their
      snow-white breasts.

      Open the pantry and give us treats,

         honor their coming
      with liquor in a flask,
      cheese in a basket,
      oat and wheat bread.

次はアーサー・シモンズの詩
題は
漂泊者の歌
俺は女達にも倦き倦きしたし
恋愛もかなり沢山になった
だが、陸（おか）が待ってる、海が待ってる
そして、夜と昼とがタップリある
ながい白い道と、灰色をした
広々とした海とが欲しいもんだ
風も吹かず、鳥も啼かず
心の痛みもやむだろう
俺はなぜ悲しみを求めたり
黄金を闘争に代えなければならないのか？
俺は随分愛しもしたし、泣きもした
だが、涙と愛とは生命じゃない
草が俺の心を、水堰が俺の血潮を
招いて叫んでいるな
日が輝き、道が照り
酒がコップに満ち溢れている
俺はかなりな智慧を蓄え
ずいぶん愉快な思いもした
だが、道は一ツ、終りも一ツ
地の涯もスグトやって来る
それから、こんどはおやすみなさい
寝床で踵と胸が痛もとままよ
ねついたら最後、長いやすらかな
ねむりだ――
醒めるにしてはあんまり深い――
寄席に五もくというものがあり、
長崎にシッポクという食い物があります。

Make offerings!—

Will you?
Or shall we leave?

Don't make us wait—

If you don't want to share,

    don't—

We'll tear off the doors and take what we wish—

    Simple to do,

Brittle ladies.

Open up! Make offerings!

The swallows are here!

We are children,

not old men.

NEXT, a recitation of an Arthur Symons poem,

    The Wanderer's Song—

    I have had enough of women,

しかし、それをダダ詩と早合点しては困ります。
牛肉とクサヤのヒモノを一緒に食ってうまいかまずいか、
たいてい見当がつきそうなものです。
ブループロ＝０
で、算盤の珠の天地を弾けば
空間そのものが出現します
そこで、淋しすぎるから、
夜店でもブラつきましょう
──無限連続

1923

20

and enough of love,
But the land *waits, and the sea waits,*
and day and night *is enough;*
Give me a long white *road,*
and the grey wide *path of the sea.*
And the wind's *will and the bird's will,*
and the heart-*ache still in me.*

Why should I seek *out sorrow,*
and give gold *for Strife?*
I have loved much and wept *much,*
but tears and love *are not life;*
The grass calls to my *heart,*
and the foam *to* my *blood cries up,*
And the sun *shines and the road* shines,
and the wine's *in the cup.*

I have had enough *of* wisdom,
and enough *of* mirth,
For the way's one and the end's one,
and it's soon *to the* ends *of the earth;*
And it's then good-night *and to bed,*
and if heels *or heart ache,*
Well, it's sound sleep and long *sleep,*
and sleep *too* deep *to* wake."

In Vaudeville, there is a tradition called the *burlesque pastiche.*

In Nagasaki, there is a dish called *shippoku.*

Despite this similarity, it is foolish to assume a relation to dada poetry.

If I chew beef and mackerel-jerky together, I generally am able to tell them apart,

and whether the mix is delicious or atrocious.

Bourgeoisie - Prolétariat = 0.

Fingering the top and bottom beads of the abacus—
an envelope of lonely space forms a round us

, here;—

...let us head to the night fair...

anywhere;—but herein

: *consecutive infinities.*

1923

【どうおなりでしょう】

あなたはどうなさいましたか
ほのおとつゆの両眼の上に
金のかつらのかんむりをつけた　しとやかなエルフィンの瞳
あなたのかおには不可思議な音楽
いままではなされなかった　一つのせいしん
あなたはどんなに　おなりでしょう

あなたは　かたく　年をおとりになるでしょう
うすい口唇にしわがよって
めにはクミチンキをおだきになって
かなしいキヲクの遺産
あなたの消え失せたオレフュ
はずかしいこっけいなものではないでしょう

たぶん　平凡な運命
結婚と出産と死

あなたののぞみのない灰色のご境遇
人生はぬすむようにすぎてゆきます

つぐなわれない空虚
むからむへ

WHAT HAS BECOME, WILL BECOME

What has become of you?
Above your eyes, reflecting flame and dew,
You placed the golden crown of woven hair—
         that highbrow elfin stare
Within the dark hymn of your face—
         the singularity of its spirit—
Until now, utterly inseparable from you,
         the self that you have grown into.

But time has hardened you unto me,
Adding a wrinkle to your thinning lips—
The flask of Tinctura Amara,
         held fast in your aging gaze—
As a bequest from our sorrow's season—
Your olives, playing dead in the garden,
         in an embarrassingly comic feat.

Perhaps for you and me, it will be
         the commonplace fate:
Of Marriage and Birth and Death—
A world of graying shades, freed from
         ulterior hopes and dreams.
Life steals itself away like a thief
Into an unredeemable vacancy—
         priceless, yes, indeed.

【無題詩】

赤ん坊よ
もっと泣け泣け
小守よ
もっと疳癪をおこせ
こわれかかった塀
つるんだトンボ

赤っ面の煙草屋の婆さん
丁寧に
十銭紙幣の皺をのばしている
五銭銅貨は五銭
十銭銅貨は十銭
梅干で酒がのめるか

破れた障子から
秋風がそよふく
バットの空箱が
アクビをかみしめる

UNTITLED I

It's a baby!
Crying as loudly as ever—
Damn little dictator!
Let his temper explode—as

      the walls collapse and
      the dragonflies mate.

Carefully,
The blushing old tobacconist lady
Smooths the wrinkles from the ten-sen bills.
A five-sen copper coin is worth five sen,
A ten-sen copper coin is worth ten sen.
Do you take liquor

      with your dried plums?

The autumn breeze whistles softly,
Through the tattered paper sliding door—
The empty baseball bat container basks

      in an endless yawn.

【無題】

港は暮れてルンペンの
のぼせ上がったたくらみは
藁で縛った乾しがれい
犬に喰わせて酒を呑む

UNTITLED II

As the port darkens, the beggar
Goes mad from the plot against his life—
Feeding his dried, straw-bound
      righteye flounder
To the dogs he drinks himself
      to sleep.

【タンカ】

雲を喰らい、霞を呑んでいるとでも
大方思っていやがるのだろう
ゴミのような雑誌に
ロハで原稿を書かせやがって
往復ハガキさえよこせば
キット返事をよこすものだと
思っていやがる　ヒョットコメ!!
おれは毎日水をガブガブと呑んで
その辺の野原から雑草をひきぬいて
ナマでムシャムシャ食っているのだが
──別段クタバリもしない
一度や二度飯が食えないと
もうふるえあがりやがって
黄色いシナビタ声を張りあげやがって
ナンダカンダと抜かしやがる
スットコドッコイのトンチキ野郎の
ヒョットコメ!!
ガツガツと、物欲しそうなそのツラは
全体なんというざまだ!!
いい気になってつけあがりやがって
やれ、ムサンケイキュウだの
ブルジョアだのと
阿保の一つ覚えみていなよまいごとを
よくあきもせず、性コリもなく
ツベコベツベコベと饒舌りやがる
デクの棒の、アヤツリ人形の
猿真似の、賤民野郎め!!

30

TANKA II

"Scarfing down clouds,

   sucking up mist..."

As a whole, I loathe the thought of *THIS,*

  just as I *LOATHE*
     the thought of *PUBLISHING*

 in *RUBBISH*

  magazines for

      FREE,
even when they *SINCERELY*

    honor

   my *EXISTENCE*

  with the return postcards
I send with my scripts—what

  an *UGLY CLOWN* face

  that is *ME!*

Every day I   *DRINK*

water and yank

WEEDS

from the field across the *STREET*...

and *MUNCH* on them *RAW*.

It doesn't particularly *KILL* me—

if I don't *EAT* once or twice

a *DAY,*

I get the shakes and *YAP*

obscenities in   *PUBLIC*

In my   *XANTHOUS,* wilted

VOICE:

"*YES,* I *am* the depraved

IDIOT knave,
     CURSED with the ugly

CLOWN FACE!"

—whose revoltingly *PIGGISH,* greedy expression

is the shame of the *EARTH*...

AND YET SEE:

the *BOURGEOISIE,*

SPOILED rotten and living in *LEISURE.*

Suddenly bereft

of *PROPERTY*

they are nothing...

NOTHING—
but desperate

whiners, tirelessly   *GRUMBLING*

and   *GRUMBLING* about

their one *LOSS* worth a *MEMORY*...

Wooden *PUPPETS,* they are—

with *MANIPULABLE*

STICKS for spines,

crudely aping

the wretched   *PROLETARIAT!*

【享楽座」のぷろろぐ】

ダダはスピノザを夢見て
いつでも「鴨緑江節」を口吟んでいる
だから　白蛇姫に恋して
宿場女郎を抱くのである

浅草の塔が火の柱になって
その灰燼から生まれたのが
青臭い"La Variete d'Epicure"なのだ
万物流転の悲哀を背負って
タンバリンとカスタネットを鳴らす
紅と白粉の子等よ！
君達の靴下の穴を気にするな‼
ひたすら「パンタライ」の呪文を唱えて
若き男達の唇と股とを祝福せよ
怪しくもいぶかしいボドビルが
そこから生まれ落ちるだろう

民衆芸術のワンタンを喰うな
月経に汚れたブルジョア娘の下着を羨むな
それはバビロニアの王者
サルダナパロスの唾棄するところだ
帝劇と有楽座を外濠に埋めて
新しい"Folly Variete"を建設しろ
かくて常に Pimp の如き
"Striking"の憧憬者　黒瀬春吉は
一夜立花家歌子の尿を飲む夢みて
「ヴリエテ」の妄想を創造した
この時　痴呆の如き色情狂者は

PROLOGUE TO "THE THEATRE OF PLEASURE"

Therefore, Dada equals Spinozan dreams, humming

      "The Tune to the River Yalu,"

falling for the Rat Snake Princess (the town

      whore he fucks).

Asakusa—cloud hat pagoda, column

of flames: from the

ashes, grass-scented *La Variété*
      d'Épicure
is born, heavy with the
sorrow attendant upon

      the flux of all things,

the beating of castanets, tambourines—

Children with lipstick, powdered faces!

Ignore the holes in your socks!
Bless the testicles and lips of the boys incanting
      Panta Rhei, Panta
Rhei!—

Origin of Vaudeville: dubious, dubitable tease.

賢くも「○○」のカツレツを吐き出して
阿片の紫衣をまとい　王者の姿に扮して
享楽座の舞台に登場するのである
畢竟　彼の「市場価値」は
正に見物の好奇心と角逐するであろう
ボオルとブリキの「平和博」が
腐れ弁天の池に吸い込まれ
山師の懐中に雨もりがして
尻に帆を揚げる滑稽を演じても
遂にその芸術的価値に於て
わが「享楽座」の茶番には及ばないのだ

虚無の大象に跨がり　毒々しい紅百合を嗅ぐ
サルダナパロスよ！
しばらく月光の下に汝の従順なピエロオと戯れろ　その時
汝の尺八は幼稚なトロイメライを奏でて　汝の胸の冷蔵庫に
秘められたドス黒い心の臓に　真赤な旋律を
点火するであろう

絶望と倦怠との餌食——
酷薄な「生命」に虐なまれる傀儡は
僅かに刹那の火花から
トマトの肌触りを［＃「肌触りを」は底本では「飢触りを」
］感じるのだ
ヒステリイの山犬よ　石油の空缶を早く乱打しろ！
そして幕をあげろ！！
ハッシュ！！　ハッショ!!

1922

Don't eat the low-brow dumplings!
Don't worship the rags of the daughters of the bourgeoisie!

King of Babylonia, Sardanapalus, limp in his den of iniquity.

Bury The Imperial Theatre and The Yurakuza Cinema in the outer-
most
> *moat of The Imperial Palace,*
> *erect a new Folly Variété!*

HARUKICHI KUROSE, pimp of ideals, ever
> plotting a workers' strike,
conceived the insane phantasm of *Variété* in a dream—

> *...drinking the piss (of Utako Tachibana).*

In opium dyed purple robes befitting a king,
> vomiting up his __ cutlet, the demented
sex fiend debuted on stage at The Theatre of Pleasure

(his "art-market" status would never match his cachet as *public*
spectacle).

As the Bowl and Tinplate "Peace Exhibition" slurps the brackish
waters of   Benten Pond,

even his comedy routine—

> *flying a sail from a seafarer's ass, pants pockets leaking—*

cannot match the farce-aesthetics of OUR "Theatre of Pleasure."

Straddling the Great Elephant of Nihility, sniffing a poison
   crimson lily,

Sardanapalus!

Moon-lit games (with *thou* loyal pierrot), as a
   puckish träumerei plays a round
in your old bamboo-flute—*play!*

   In the dusky
   bowels of his heart, in the refrigerated cage
   of her chest,

   a reddish tune is set ablaze.

To the victims of boredom and despair—

   "The puppet, in unkindly fate, knows for
   a moment's spark, what it is to be
   a tomato—"

(In the original draft, "to be" had been "to be hungry for.")

Deranged pack of wolves!
       Drum on the kerosene cans!
Raise the curtains!

Hush! Shush!

         1922

ACKNOWLEDGEMENTS

Thank you to the places where these translations appeared first: *The Brooklyn Rail, Fence, The New Republic,* and *Puerto del Sol.*

「煩悶を露にせよ」